MW01001623

Study Guide

A Prayer for Owen Meany

BookCaps™ Study Guide

www.bookcaps.com

Table of Contents

Historic Context

John Irving was born in Exeter, New Hampshire in 1942. He spent most of his time while growing up at Philips Exeter Academy where his stepfather worked as a teacher. Despite being dyslexic Irving became very passionate about reading and writing, which became his calling in life. He studied in Vienna at the Institute for European Studies under the tutelage of, famous novelist, Gunter Grass. After returning to the United States, Irving was honored to study at the Writer's Workshop at the University of Iowa where he took on Kurt Vonnegut as a mentor. Once he completed his high education studies, Irving became a teacher at Mount Holyoke College and soon began writing novels.

Though Irving has produced many successful novels, "A Prayer for Owen Meany" (1989) has been widely considered as his finest. It has also been considered his most autobiographical; while the character of Owen Meany is entirely fictional, the historical events of the time are accurate and the setting and some characters of the novel come almost directly out of Irving's life. John Wheelwright is a direct reflection of John Irving himself; he has never met his father, his stepfather is an educator, he works at an all-girls school, and he is dyslexic. Irving writes in a style which includes plots which are fantastical and characters that will be remembered and loved by readers. Though critics have not always considered Irving an important writer in terms of his artistic flair, his works have been widely appreciated well-received by readers.

Plot

John Wheelwright is living in Canada in 1987. He is the narrator of a story about his childhood, his friendship with Owen Meany, and his experiences with religion peppered with entries about his disgust for the American political system in the 1980s. John grew up in Gravesend, New Hampshire raised by his mother Tabby, her boyfriend-turned-husband Dan Needham, and his grandmother Mrs. Wheelwright. Owen Meany is a boy who is extraordinarily small, has an exceptionally high-pitched voice, and who is loved by everyone. When John is eleven his mother is killed by the only baseball that Owen Meany ever hit, when it goes foul and hits her in the head. John and Owen remain friends, and John begins to realize exactly how remarkable Owen is.

When Owen believes that he foresees his own death and the date that will happen he becomes obsessed with getting to that point in his life, while leaving his mark on others in the process. The boys attend Gravesend Academy together where Owen excels academically and socially, and where he stirs the pot with his political and religious views. Despite always being against the war, Owen knows that he needs to join the military because that is how he will die. When John is in graduate school Owen, helps him to dodge the draft by cutting off his trigger finger and then asks John to visit him in Phoenix. John witnesses Owen's death as a hero, just the way Owen always knew he would die. Owen's life and death helps John to realize that some things in life are truly miraculous, such as Owen's existence.

Themes

Religion

At the very beginning of the novel, John mentions to the reader that the reason he is a Christian is because of Owen Meany, and he has gone between different branches of Christianity various times in his life. The entire novel is spent telling the reader why Owen Meany had such a profound religious effect on the narrator. Owen believes that he is an instrument of God, and he has been put on the Earth to do God's work in certain situations; such as when Reverend Merrill prayed briefly for Tabby to die and immediately after Owen hit a foul ball that snapped her neck and killed her.

Fate and Free Will

From the time that Owen Meany is a young boy, he believes that his life is for a purpose, and it is his fate to live his life in the pattern that God has set out for him. Owen believes that he is a product of Immaculate Conception, as his parents told him, and because of this he is an instrument of God and serves a greater purpose in life than some other people may. Owen foresees the exact date of his death, he knows that he will be in the military when it happens; he knows he will die saving Vietnamese children accompanied by nuns, and he knows that he will die in Phoenix. While others try to deny that Owen is an instrument of God, it seems a pretty powerful argument that he is.

Friendship

The friendship between John and Owen truly lasts through anything, which is obvious when they remain friends after Owen, basically, kills John's mother. John and Owen are two very different people who seem to mesh into a perfect union of friendship. Even when John is pretty sure that Owen is crazy, after fully believing he is an instrument of God and knows the exact day and circumstances which pertain to his death, John sticks by Owen's side. Owen saves John from the draft and helps him to find out who he is; in return John helps Owen achieve his ultimate destiny.

Family

The family dynamic is complicated in this novel and pretty nontraditional in some ways. John is close to both his Wheelwright family as well as the Eastman side of his family, but he does not know who his father is until the end of the novel. The two people who John is closest to and are the most like his family are Dan, his stepfather, and Owen, who is like a brother to him. Owen seems to consider the Wheelwrights his family as he spends most of his time at their home rather than with his own parents, whom he has an odd relationship with.

The Past

John Wheelwright, as the narrator in 1987, is stuck in the past and has never stopped praying for Owen Meany to be given back to him. Other characters who are in John's life as an adult point out that he needs to leave the past behind him because he has a hard time letting things go. Often when he is talking about events that are happening in current American politics, such as with the Reagan administration which John hates, it makes him remember Owen and his childhood. It seems that the past and the events of the past are the only things that keep John going in the present.

Identity

John searches for his identity just as any child does while growing up, but he wonders what parts of his identity come from his father whom he has never met. It is not only John's identity that is explored; it is the identity of John's unknown father and also the identity of John's mother who seems to have lived a double life, which are explored. When John finds out who his father is he is actually disappointed and finds the man to be spineless, not at all what he expected. In addition, when he finds out about his mother's life in Boston he is tortured and confused by the fact that she hid it from him.

Principles

Owen is not shy in sharing his views and his principles with the world, even as a child. He has very strong opinions on how people should act and whether or not they live up to expectations, and he shares these opinions freely. When Owen begins writing for The Grave newspaper in high school he earns the pseudonym "THE VOICE" for writing columns on any and everything that matters and his opinion on such matters. He is especially passionate about John F. Kennedy's campaign and subsequent election, and also about the Vietnam War which he becomes obsessed with joining because he feels it is his destiny and purpose.

Appearance

As a narrator, John Wheelwright describes the
appearances of the people in his life very specifically,
from Hester's strong jaw to Reverend Merrill's
hairline. The character whose appearance stands out
the most, of course, is Owen Meany. Owen is
extremely small for his age even as an adult he does
not make five feet tall, he has a sharp and distinct
nose and prominent ears which stuck out from the
side of his head. He is so pale his skin is almost
translucent; John describes him as almost looking like
a rodent but more so resembling an old man even as a
boy. Owen's appearance sets the tone that he is truly
one of a kind.

Faith vs. Doubt

Owen always has very strong religious views and a belief in God, though his own views are of religion are quite distinct and strict to whom Owen is as a person. Owen never doubts anything in life as he feels God has a purpose for everyone and for every action; he feels terrible for his part in Tabby's death, but he knows that it is all part of a plan that has already been formed. When John is a child his own religious beliefs mainly come from what Owen does or says, because John has no real beliefs of his own. John judges his faith on which church and Reverend he likes better. Reverend Merrill, though a clergyman, bases his faith on doubt; he believes that since there is little to no proof of a God then faith is necessary.

Sacrifice

Because of Owen's faith and his belief that he was a Virgin Birth, he is willing to make any sacrifices that he feels are in God's plans for him. Owen knows that he was sent to the Earth to be an instrument of God and act out God's plans, such as the death of Tabby Wheelwright and the death of Mr. Fish's dog. He foresees how he will die and makes moves in his life to ensure that he gets himself to that specific day, time, and location. Owen makes sacrifices wherever he sees fit because he knows that it is his destiny to die as a hero, having acted out God's will.

Characters

John Wheelwright

John is the narrator of the novel and the best friend of Owen Meany. John is very close to his mother and his grandmother, and he does not know who his father is until the end of the novel. He grows up in Gravesend, New Hampshire, and he has no particular religious beliefs of his own until he becomes close with Owen. After Owen's death, John becomes a believer of faith and destiny, and he decides, in 1987 to write the story of his and Owen's friendship and Owen's death. As an adult John is bitter and angry about his experiences and losses, and he often blames his troubles on the Reagan administration.

Owen Meany

Owen is John's best friend and is an honorary member of John's family. He is a dwarf with very distinct features and a high-pitched voice; the voice teacher in Boston tells Owen that his larynx is always stuck in the screaming position. Owen has a very powerful personality and is loved and respected by nearly everyone he meets. His strong principles and opinions on any and everything earn him the nickname "THE VOICE" when he writes for The Grave newspaper in high school. Owen believes that he is an instrument of God and has been put on the planet to act out God's plan.

Tabitha Wheelwright

Tabitha, or Tabby, is John Wheelwright's mother. She is an incredibly beautiful woman and serves as an idealistic image of what a mother should be, mostly for Owen who has quite the crush on her. Tabby says that she got pregnant by a man she met on the train to Boston though she never reveals his identity to anyone, though John does find out that his father is Reverend Merrill toward the end of the novel. Tabby was killed when John was eleven by a foul ball which broke her neck, and which happened to be hit by Owen Meany.

Hester Eastman

Hester is the cousin of John Wheelwright and is less than one year older than him. Hester was a very sexual person even as a young girl and would often play games which involved her touching the crotch of boys to "tag" them or making John kiss her if he lost the game. John had a crush on Hester, despite her being his cousin, and was disappointed when she started dating Owen. Hester is determined to stay with Owen through his eccentricities and despite the fact that he knows he will die soon. She, like John, is forever damaged and traumatized by Owen's death.

Harriet Wheelwright

Harriet Wheelwright is John's maternal grandmother. She lives at 80 Front Street, which is the setting for many events of the novel. She is very prominent and domineering, coming from an aristocratic family which counted John Adams as an ancestor, though she is quite loving as well especially of John and Owen. She married into the family which founded Gravesend, and as she gets older she becomes known as the matriarch of the town. She serves as Owen's benefactor for his school supplies and clothing, and he feels as though he let her down when he is expelled.

Dan Needham

Dan Needham is the husband of Tabby Wheelwright. Tabby meets Dan on a train to Boston, the same place she claims to have met John's father, when John is six. Dan is a theater director and history teacher at Gravesend Academy. He and Tabby are together for four years before they are married and Tabby dies only one year later. After Tabby's death, Dan remains in John's life as a father-figure, and he helps Mrs. Wheelwright to raise John as though he were his own child. Dan, although not a biological father, is the epitome of what a father should be.

Reverend Merrill

Reverend Merrill is the minister at the Congregational Church in Gravesend. He teaches a theory of faith based on doubt, because there is little to no proof that God really exists and where there is doubt there must be faith. Reverend Merrill tends to be bitter and skeptical which John later learns is because he feels responsible for Tabby's death. Rev. Merrill is John's biological father, and he is the person that Tabby was waving to in the stands when she got hit with the baseball. Just before she was hit Rev. Merrill had said a short prayer wishing that Tabby would die.

Reverend Wiggin

Reverend Wiggin is the rector of the Episcopalian Church. He is married to a woman named Barb and is an incredibly brash and somewhat ridiculous man. Reverend Wiggin was a pilot before he took his place in the church. He prefers to quote Bible verses, which are outlandish and not often read in other churches, and John finds him to be a bit of a joke. When Tabby and Dan are married they begin to attend Reverend Wiggin's church rather than Reverend Merrill's because it is the church which Dan prefers.

Barb Wiggin

Barb Wiggin is the wife of Reverend Wiggin and a former stewardess. She is brash and ridiculous, just as her husband, and also has a bit of a malicious streak. She and Owen Meany did not see eye-to-eye on certain matters regarding the Christmas Pageant of 1953, so she found it entertaining to press Owen against her chest and kiss him on the mouth, giving him an erection, while he was swaddled as the Baby Jesus. She later insisted that Owen be forbidden to enter the church ever again but took it back when Dan threatened to expose her for endangering another child.

Martha Eastman

Martha Eastman is the sister of Tabby Wheelwright. She is the mother of Hester, Simon, and Noah and is married to Alfred. John thinks that Martha has always been a bit jealous of Tabby because Tabby was prettier and a better singer. Martha is the only person who frowned on Tabby's frivolous affair with John's father because everyone else thought she was perfect. John stays with Martha and her family occasionally in Sawyer Depot where he works at the lumber yard and goes skiing with his cousins.

Noah and Simon Eastman

Noah and Simon are Hester's brothers, John's cousins, and Martha's sons. Both boys attend Gravesend Academy and were rather wild and reckless during their younger years. After graduating from Gravesend, both boys attend colleges on the West Coast. John was pretty terrified of the boys when he was younger because they liked to roughhouse and were outgoing, but it added some excitement to his life that he did not have when they weren't around.

Mr. Fish

Mr. Fish lives next door to Harriet Wheelwright. Mr. Fish has a dog named Sagamore which he loves very much; he is greatly saddened when Sagamore is killed by a diaper truck which struck him while he was chasing a football punted by Owen Meany. Mr. Fish finds enjoyment acting in the plays put on by the Gravesend Players, an acting troupe led by Dan Needham. Mr. Fish is always around but remains mysterious, as no one seems to know much about him. Owen and John play catch with him sometimes, and they are curious about his life too.

Dick Jarvits

Dick Jarvits is the fifteen-year-old brother of a soldier who has died in the war. Owen has the job of notifying the families of fallen soldiers, and this is how the two meet. Dick Jarvits is a large boy who carries a machete with him at all times; he arrives at the airport where Owen is seeing John off and throws a grenade into a group of Vietnamese boys because he dreams of killing the Viet Cong. Owen smothers the grenade with his own body and dies as a hero; Dick Jarvits is killed with his own machete by Major Rawls.

Mr. Randy White

Mr. White is the headmaster at the school Owen and John attend, Gravesend Academy. Mr. White and Owen do not get along, mostly because of Owen's column in The Grave, in which his byline reads, "THE VOICE". Mr. White is staunchly republican, compared to Owen's democratic leanings and support of Kennedy. Mr. White is furious when Owen implements two pranks, which involve a Volkswagen and a disembodied statue of Mary Magdalene being displayed in the school auditorium; he works to have Owen expelled just before he is set to graduate as valedictorian.

Mr. and Mrs. Meany

Mr. and Mrs. Meany are the parents of Owen Meany. Owen has a mysterious relationship with his parents. John learns from Owen that the Catholic Church as insulted his parents in some way, but he does not learn how until after Owen's death. When Owen was eleven, his parents told him that he was a virgin birth, which led Owen to believe that he was an instrument of God. Mr. Meany owns the stone quarry in town and Mrs. Meany spends most of her time alone in the house.

Chapter Summary

Chapter One

The narrator of the novel is John Wheelwright, and he tells the reader that he will never forget Owen Meany. Though John could remember Owen because of his small stature and strained voice, or because John's mother's death was at Owen's inadvertent hands, the real reason he will always remember Owen Meany is because he made John believe in God. John has switched faiths several times throughout his life but considers himself loyal to Christianity and reads his prayer-book often. He wishes to have his body shipped to the United States from Canada, where he has been living, when he dies so he can be buried next to his mother. He states that the faith he does carry is because of Owen Meany.

John remembers knowing Owen Meany during his childhood. Owen was underdeveloped, even in his vocal chords which made his voice strained and quiet. In Sunday school, he was often passed around the room over the heads of the other students who loved him; the girls considered him as one of their dolls. The Sunday school teacher, Mrs. Walker, would often blame Owen when she would enter the room and find it in disarray, but Owen never complained; he never even complained when he would be hung from his locker by the bigger kids at school.

John grew up in Gravesend, New Hampshire where the Wheelwright name is something of legend and aristocracy. His maternal grandmother was descended from John Adams and his ancestor, another John Wheelwright, founded the town. This other John Wheelwright had been expelled from Massachusetts for having unorthodox religious beliefs, and the narrator believes that could he where his own religious wavering comes into play. John's mother was a Wheelwright, and he was born with her last name; he never knew his father and she never spoke of him. One day when John and Owen were throwing rocks into the river Owen, whose little arms were not strong enough for his rocks to actually make it to the river, told John that someday he will learn of his father if not during life then in the afterlife. After making this statement, Owen surprised both of them by throwing a rock way out into the river, securing John's belief in God.

John tells the reader that the two main industries in Gravesend are lumber and rock; the Wheelwrights dealt in lumber while the Meany family owned the quarry. The only thing that John knew of his mother's pregnancy was that she had met a man on the train on her way to Boston; the only person who looked down on her for this was her sister Martha, everyone accepted everything that John's mother did because she was a beautiful and caring person. One time when John, Owen, and some other kids were swimming in the quarry Owen hid in a crack between two rocks to make the other kids think he had drown, and when no one came looking for him or seemed concerned, he told them all off for leaving him to die.

John and Owen talk about religion and John finds that Owen has very specific beliefs and is very passionate about them. Owen also has a crush on John's mother, who wants Owen's family to send him to private school because she feels that he is quite special. One day when John and Owen were eleven years old they were playing baseball and Owen hit a ball for the first time; the ball went foul and John's mother in the head, killing her. John recalls chaos happening around him and Owen disappearing; John suspects that Owen kept the ball.

Chapter Two

John's mother was named Tabitha but everyone
called her Tabby. She was very good looking and
everyone seemed to want to be near her and to touch
her, like a cat; her response was cat-like as well
because sometimes she evaded it and sometimes she
reveled in it. John thinks that she must have flirted
with men, though he had never seen her do it, because
she met his father on the Boston and Maine railroad
and she also met Dan Needham there. Dan Needham
married Tabby and converted her and John from the
Congregational Church to the Episcopalian Church.
When John met Dan, he was surprised to see that he
was young-looking and red-headed which was quite a
change from the men Tabby usually dated. Dan, a
newly hired History teacher at Gravesend Academy,
gave John a paper bag and told him not to look in it
but to make sure it did not move. John looked in the
bag and was horrified at the monster he saw there; it
ended up being a stuffed armadillo that John soon fell
in love with and so did Owen.

John used to visit his Aunt Martha and Uncle Alfred,
as well as their three children Noah, Simon, and
Hester, in the White Mountains. He was intimidated
by his cousins because they had lived a much
different and more athletic life than he had. When
they would go skiing, he would fall often, and Hester,
who is less than one year older than John and is
obsessed with sex, would tell him to be careful, or he
would go sterile. They would often play competitive
games with one another, which John found exciting,
especially because of the sexual tension he was

starting to experience with Hester. Within the next few years, she would often intimidate the girlfriends of her brothers and have sex with all of their friends. John remembers that when they were kids the punishment for losing games would be to kiss Hester, and after a while, he would lose on purpose.

On Thanksgiving one year the cousins came to John's grandmother's house on Front Street, and John worried how they would react to Owen; he had nothing to worry about because they loved him. Playing hide and seek one day Hester would grab the boys' "doinks" before they found her, in order to win, but in Owen's case she just tickled him which caused him to pee his pants. Owen ran away horrified, but John and his grandmother found Owen and convinced him to come back. After Owen inadvertently killed John's mother he left all of his baseball cards on John's front porch, which Dan told John he should give back to show Owen he still loves him; John gave back the baseball cards and also sent the armadillo over. When John received the armadillo back, he was upset to find that Owen had cut its claws off. Later, he finds out that Owen was sending a message; God used Owen's hands as an instrument to take John's mother, so God has taken his hands; he is an instrument of God. John recalls discussing the Vietnam War with Owen when they were in their senior year of high school; Owen seemed to understand the war perfectly and often criticized it. It was Owen who gave John the idea to move to Canada to evade the war and so he did in 1971. He believes that Owen gave him much more than he ever took from him.

Chapter Three

John recalls that his mother was a seamstress and used to keep a dummy next to her bed, which she often draped in fine clothing from stores in Boston, which she replicated herself before returning the clothes to the store. John and Owen would sometimes dress the dummy, and every now and then Tabby would wear the outfits that they created; the one thing in her closet she only wore once is the only thing that was not black or white: a red dress. The red dress is something that Tabby wore in a play which Dan was producing in Gravesend, and the only play that she was ever in.

One night when Owen was staying at John's he woke feverish and went to tell Tabby, but he soon came back to John's room crying that he had seen an angel next to her bed. John went to look and saw only the dummy, assuming this was what Owen had seen, though he insisted the angel was on the opposite side of the bed. John feels that because Owen was running a fever he had hallucinated, but Owen later believes he interrupted fate. He thinks that the angel was the angel of death coming for Tabby, and he interrupted, which is why it was his baseball that killed her not long after. Owen slept in Tabby's room that night just in case the angel came back, but it did not.

It was four years of dating before Tabby and Dan were actually married, despite the fact that Dan was accepted easily by the Wheelwrights and the community. It was not a matter of religion, either, because both the Congregational Church and the

Episcopalian Church accepted the couple. John preferred Reverend Merrill of the Congregational Church to Reverend Wiggins of the Episcopalian Church, though Owen did not like Reverend Merrill much. Despite John's preference his family began to attend the Episcopalian Church; though, both Reverends ended up presiding over Tabby and Dan's nuptials. The wedding took place in the nondenominational church at Gravesend Academy, and that is the same church Tabby's funeral took place the following year.

The wedding reception was at John's grandmother's house where people commented that Owen's dark suit made it look like he was going to a funeral. During the reception, Hester peed in the bushed so she would not have to wait in line and she gave, an embarrassed, Owen her underpants to hold onto while she went; he stuffed them into his pocket. As Dan and Tabby prepared to leave the reception to head out on their honeymoon, a storm started brewing. They agreed to drop Owen off at his house on their way, and he left with Hester's underpants still in his pocket. Hester was the only one who knew, but when it started to rain Hester's yellow dress became see-through, and everyone found out she was wearing no underpants, and she ran away humiliated.

John recalls all of the people who played a part in the baseball game the day his mother died. The coach who had told Owen to hit the ball and felt responsible for the death was suffering from Alzheimer's; the boy who struck out just before Owen came to bat had been killed in Vietnam; and the boy who was on base when Owen hit the ball had died in a car crash after evading Vietnam with his drug use. At the funeral, Owen kept telling people he was sorry, and, after the funeral, he took the dummy from Dan's apartment because he knew that seeing it would drive Dan crazy. Owen keeps the dummy at his own house, and it wears the red dress. In February of 1987 while John is writing from his home in Toronto he states that he now believes in angels.

Chapter Four

Christmas 1953 is John's first Christmas without his mother and John and Owen decide to go through the dormitories at Gravesend Academy with the key John stole from Dan. Dan works on a production of A Christmas Carol and John and Owen are expected to participate in the church's Christmas pageant. As the boys snoop through the dormitories of the students they quickly learn where the pornography is stashed; as soon as they find pornography in a boys room Owen loses respect for the boy in question. They find condoms in the room of one boy and decide to try the condoms on their own "tiny penises". Owen is gleeful that condoms are outlawed by the Catholic Church and obviously sees putting one on as a stab in the direction of Catholicism; he is constantly trying to repay the Church for an unknown insult that the Church delivered to his parents.

When the members of the Episcopal Church meet to cast for the Christmas pageant, Owen adamantly refuses to play the role of the Announcing angel, as he has been made to play for the past few years. He suggests that he instead play the role of Baby Jesus, an idea which is accepted. Owen asks that he be allowed to create his own sort of nest, rather than be subjected to lying in a crib, using "Away in the Manger" to cite textual references to support his argument. He even suggests that the girl playing Mary bow to him, an adjustment which is kept in the pageant. John, in 1987, thinks about the church he attends and how he only goes to weekday services because he does not like to be there with children who are forced to attend on weekends. He also does not attend Christmas pageants anymore because the only in 1953 was enough for him, as that was the day he witnessed a miracle.

Dan's "A Christmas Carol" was a flop because of the amateur actors. Mr. Fish, the neighbor to John's grandmother, had played Scrooge. John recalls the day that Mr. Fish's dog Sagamore had died. Owen had punted a football and Sagamore chased it into the road where he was struck and killed by a diaper truck. Owen presided over the burial of the dog and recited a Bible verse while John's mother held his hand. Before the pageant, John visited Owen's home, which is something that he rarely did. He notices a mangled-looking nativity scene on the mantle and tells Mrs. Meany that Owen is playing the Baby Jesus, which she is shocked by. Mrs. Meany, for the first time, tells John she is sorry about his mother's death, as she scrutinizes the dummy which is still in Owen's room.

Owen and John are exploring the Waterhouse Hall dorms one day when they hear another key in the lock. A couple by the name of Brinker-Smith enters the room, and John and Owen hide. The Brinker-Smiths are members of the faculty who have recently given birth to twins; Ginger Brinker-Smith is a bit of a sex-symbol at the Academy. The couple immediately falls onto one of the dormitory beds and begins to have sex, obviously enjoying the time away from their babies. The boys are shocked at what they are witnessing, and Owen decides that sex makes people crazy. When it is time for Dan's play, the

Ghost of Christmas Yet to Come quits so Owen offers himself for the job. Owen becomes a bit of a legend amongst the townspeople, as he has now been cast as both Baby Jesus and the Ghost of Christmas Yet to Come.

Chapter Five

John thinks that Owen's performance as the Ghost of Christmas Yet to Come during rehearsals is too ominous and may hurt the tone of the play; he is relieve when Owen comes down with the sniffles because he thinks a cold will affect Owen's performance for the better. Mr. Fish accompanies John and Owen to the church the day of the pageant; though he is not a churchgoer he is intrigued to see Owen as the Baby Jesus. As the boys are getting ready for the pageant, Owen insists that he put on his lucky scarf before he is swaddled. Owen and Barb Wiggin argue for a bit, but eventually she picks him up and carries him to the manger where she presses him up against her breasts and kisses him full on the mouth before putting him down, for luck. As Barb lowers Owen into his nest, John can see that Owen has an erection. Owen manages to get himself under control before the pageant begins, and he gives Barb a scathing look. From that moment, the pageant goes steadily downhill culminating when Owen sees his parents in the audience and yells "What do you think you're doing here?" As Owen's parents leave he instructs John and the Virgin Mary to carry him outside and into his parents truck; everyone follows them outside and watches in awe of what is happening.

John recounts that the nativity scene that Christmas has changed his view of the Christmas story for him, and in his mind Owen Meany is the Baby Jesus. He recalls everyone filing back into the church, confused and Mr. Fish complimenting Reverend Wiggin on the "primitive" display and the inventiveness of the performance. Dan sees that a boy is still hanging from a pulley above the stage, as Barb Wiggin has forgotten about him. As Barb yells that Owen is to never step foot in the church again Dan tells her to rethink this decision or he will be forced to tell that she left a boy hanging from a pulley; she concedes. That Christmas Eve is the first one John spent without his mother and the first he spent in Gravesend as they had always stayed with Aunt Martha and her family each year before. John and his grandmother attend the performance of A Christmas Carol that Christmas Eve. John asks Owen about his reaction to seeing his parents at the pageant, and Owen makes a vague reference to the "insult" which his parents faced at the hands of the Catholic Church. As John looks out into the audience, he sees many people who were at the baseball field the night his mother died. He remembers his mother waving to someone before she was hit, though he does not know who the person was; he imagines it was his father.

During the play, Owen has to bring Scrooge, played by Mr. Fish to visit his own grave. Upon reaching the grave Owen suddenly cries out in terror and leaves the stage, refusing to come back out. When John goes to see what happened Owen tells him that he read his own name on the tombstone. Reverend Merrill drives the boys home, and when John reaches his grandmother's house he knows something is wrong. He enters the house and learns that Lydia, his grandmother's maid, has died. When Mrs. Wheelwright returns home and learns of Lydia's death she thinks that somehow Owen knew it was going to happen but confused it with his own death, and that is why he was scared at the play. John is forced to share a room with Germaine, another maid, that evening and he finds that he is sexually attracted to her despite only being eleven. After she falls asleep, he calls Owen and tells him everything he has been thinking that night. Owen agrees that Tabby could have been waving to John's dad and wants to help John find him. In addition, he tells John that he thinks the lustful feelings he was having for Germaine must have come from his father's side. Owen disagrees that he may have foreseen Lydia's death and confused it with his own because he saw "the whole thing" which John knows means Owen saw the date too. John asks Owen what the date said, and Owen tells him there was no date; John cries because he knows that Owen is lying.

Chapter Six

John's grandmother decides to purchase a television after Lydia dies. She has strong opinions on everything that is on television and John and Owen find they have a hard time finding it interesting without her running commentary. Owen and Mrs. Wheelwright both develop a love for Liberace and John thinks that they are crazy to the point of speaking to Dan about it. Dan tells John not to be so judgmental and snobbish; Mrs. Wheelwright is old, and Owen has not yet fully developed intellectually as he will when he gets in to Gravesend Academy. Owen receives a full scholarship to Gravesend when it is time to go but John is recommended another year of public school first; Owen decides to stay in public school for a year as well so he and John can stay in the same grade.

By 1957, it is just about time for the boys to be ready to enter Gravesend Academy. The boys attend performances of the Gravesend Players and try to remember which people in the audience were around on the day Tabby died. Owen still wants to help John find his father, so he tells him that every time he gets an erection to think about whether he reminds himself of anyone that he knows. John wishes that he had seen Hester more when he was younger, but Owen reminds him that Hester is his cousin, so it is probably a good thing that he does not see more of her. In 1958, the boys get their drivers licenses, and they drive to the beach together to check out girls. Girls are starting to find Owen attractive now, as he has begun to develop muscle tone and he smokes

Camels.

In Fall 1958, the boys start attending Gravesend Academy where Owen achieves instant popularity for being sarcastic and cool. He is dubbed "THE VOICE" for the essays he writes in the school paper, The Grave, which are penned in all capital letters. Owen invites Hester to a school dance which Simon and Noah think is a terrible idea because she will leave Owen to have sex with someone else, but they prove to be inseparable the whole time; there are even rumors that they slept together after the dance. That summer Owen breaks a guys' finger defending himself and becomes "untouchable" by reputation; he also keeps dating Hester who is now in college, which makes his reputation soar even higher. Owen develops a love for basketball and practices a move where John holds him up, so he can dunk the ball, though John is not too keen on the stunt.

Owen gets into some heated arguments with Reverend Merrill, who teaches a religious philosophy based on doubt at the Academy, and the new headmaster Randy White who is staunchly republican. Owen is a big supporter of Kennedy and White supports Nixon, which causes quite the clash. Owen is ecstatic when Kennedy wins the election and finds his speech inspirational; looking back on that time John finds it inspirational as well, especially considering his hatred for the Reagan administration in 1987.

Chapter Seven

John and Owen are nineteen years old and in their senior year at Gravesend Academy when Owen explains to John why he cut the armadillo's claws off; John thinks that Owen is insane to imagine himself as an instrument of God. One of the biggest arguments that the boys have that year is about college; Owen is set to be valedictorian of the class and has been accepted to Yale and Harvard and John is planning to attend the University of New Hampshire. Owen wants John to apply to an Ivy League school, or he wants to attend UNH with John because he has received a full scholarship there for academic excellence. John does not want Owen to sell himself short for the sake of them going to the same school though.

Because the boys are senior they have the privilege of taking a train into Boston twice a week and rather than party like most of the seniors do, Owen takes John to a clothing store called Jerrold's. It turns out that Jerrold's was the name on the label of the red dress that Tabby had owned, though she had lied and said the store burned down many years before which is why she still owned the dress. After seeing a photo of Tabby, the proprietor of the store referred to her as "The Lady in Red", a lounge singer during the 1940s-1950s. John is baffled and numb by this information and cannot fathom why his mother lied to him. They are sent to see her voice teacher Graham McSwiney who also refers to her as "The Lady in Red" and as a lazy student. He gives the boys the names of a couple men who were associated with the lounge, The Orange Grove, where Tabby sang before it closed.

John interjects frequently to comment on the state of American politics in 1987, and how much he despises Reagan and everything he is doing; American is currently in the midst of the Iran-Contra scandal. His rage always reminds him of Vietnam and the multitude of facts he knows about that war. He thinks of the New Year's Eves that he spent with Hester and Owen discussing the war and lives lost.

In 1961 Mrs. Wheelwright got Owen a journal which he wrote in about everything: dreams, premonitions, and Kennedy mostly. Owen never let John see the diary though the 1987-version of John has seen it and occasionally adds snippets of it into the narrative. Owen is still involved in a constant struggle with Mr. White, who tries to have Owen expelled after he makes a sexual advance toward another student's mother in an attempt to get her to stop talking about Kennedy's affair with Marilyn Monroe. Owen is not expelled but is placed on probation and forced to visit with psychologist Dr. Dolder. Sometimes Owen visits with Reverend Merrill also to talk about Dr. Dolder and also about the afterlife. One day when Owen gets to school early to set up the kitchen for breakfast (one of his jobs as a scholarship student) he finds that Dr. Dolder has drunkenly left his car in Owen's parking spot, as he was drinking with Mr. White the night before. Owen recruits the basketball team to move Dr. Dolder's Volkswagen Beetle into the auditorium. Mr. White discovers the prank before the morning meeting and asks some teachers to help him move the car back; however, the teachers are not strong enough, and the car is damaged and Mr. White is pinned beneath it. Owen is expelled after this incident, combined with the discovery that he had made fake IDs for some students earlier that year.

Owen apologizes to Mrs. Wheelwright because he feels he let her down, and he asks her to make sure Dan and John both attend the morning meeting the next day. They are worried about Owen and try to find him that night, but they have no luck. At school, the next morning, they see that a statue of Mary Magdalene from the Catholic School has been moved into the auditorium and is missing a head and arms. Rev. Merrill leads everyone in a prayer for Owen, as Owen has asked him to do, as Mr. White tries to move the statue himself. Mr. White runs off, and he is voted out as headmaster of Gravesend. Owen receives a diploma from the public high school, and his acceptances to Harvard and Yale are revoked; he decides to attend UNH but has lost his scholarship, so he enrolls in the ROTC program to foot the bill. At this point, there are just over 11,000 troops in Vietnam, and none are in combat. John recalls that if he had read Owen's diary back then he would have prayed for him harder; Owen states in the journal that he knew when he would die and then had a dream showing him how he would die. When John does get to read it, he finds out that what Owen saw on the tombstone during the play was "1LT PAUL O. MEANY, JR." Paul is Owen's real first name, and 1LT means First Lieutenant.

Chapter Eight

The summer of 1962 Owen and John spend in different places; John works at the lumberyard with Simon and Noah in Sawyer's Depot and Owen works at his father's quarry. John cannot lose his virginity despite the many dates he has been set up on by his cousins, and Owen has been living with Hester. They correspond with one another through letters, and when Marilyn Monroe dies Owen blames Kennedy for treating her as nothing more than a "cheap thrill" as most politicians treat America as a whole. When the boys begin their classes at UNH John excels academically while Owen struggles.

The summer of 1963 John works for Owen's father engraving tombstones. That year Kennedy is assassinated which upsets Mrs. Wheelwright and Owen works to build a new Mary Magdalene statue. As time passes, more men are sent to Vietnam and Hester becomes increasingly angry about the war, especially as Owen becomes more and more determined to be a part of it. John and Hester do not understand Owen's persistence and John tells Owen's ROTC officer that he does not think Owen is mentally stable. Owen, however, just feels as though he needs to see the war to understand it.

After the boys finish their junior year of college Owen starts to worry that because he is small he will be given a desk job, and John starts to worry that he will be drafted though he will be saved for a short amount of time by going to graduate school. Eventually Owen admits to John that he believes his destiny is to die in Vietnam because he had a dream that he rescued some Vietnamese children and then died in a nun's arms; John again thinks that Owen is crazy. John is safe from the draft until just after his first year of graduate school when he receives a notice to report to the draft board for a physical. He does not know what to do, and Owen tells him to do nothing, but to just wait for him to arrive. When Owen arrives he tells John to meet him at his father's monument shop. At the shop, Owen gives John a couple of beers and tells him that he is going to cut off the index finger of John's right hand; if he has no trigger finger he will not be drafted. John watches his blood spatter on Owen's goggles as Owen tells him to think of this act as a gift.

Chapter Nine

In 1987, Hester is a famous rock star known as Hester the Molester. John hates her music but his students love it and sometimes he takes them to her concerts to go backstage and meet her. Hester tells the girls that John is a virgin, which they disbelieve, but he confirms that what he has experienced has made him uninterested in sex. John says that Hester was hurt very badly by Owen's death because she loved him immensely. John has been visited by Owen's spirit twice since he has died; once was at Dan's house on Front Street, which used to be Mrs. Wheelwright's until she died. The experience was so frightful for John that the roots of his hair turned white. John visits Dan every August and Dan tries to convince John to move back because it has been twenty years since Owen died, but he cannot bring himself to do it.

In the summer of 1968, just after Owen's death, he went to the Meany house to talk to Mr. Meany about the funeral arrangements. He finds that, in Owen's room, Mary Magdalene's arms have been stuck onto his mother's dummy. John goes through Owen's things to find the baseball that killed his mother, but he cannot. Mr. Meany tells John that Owen was immaculately conceived, which they told Owen when he was eleven, and the insult against them from the Catholic Church was their disbelief. Mr. Meany shows John the tombstone that Owen made for himself six months before he died, which appears exactly as the one Owen saw during the play, and which has the exact date of his real death on it. John hates Owen's parents for allowing him to believe he is the second-coming of Christ. Reverend Merrill agrees with John when they discuss it. John suddenly remembers see Rev. Merrill in the bleachers the day his mother died, and then he feels Owen's presence. Owen's voice comes out of Rev. Merrill telling John to look in one of his drawers. John finds the baseball that killed his mother and knows that Rev. Merrill is his father and is the person Tabby was waving to that day. The Reverend admits he is John's father and that he had briefly wished for Tabby to die that day; immediately after she was struck with the baseball. Reverend Merrill felt responsible for her death and lost his faith that day. John hates Reverend Merrill for being spineless and that night throws the baseball through the Reverend's window and places the dummy on the front lawn, which Rev. Merrill thinks is a sign from Tabby. His faith never again wavers.

In July 1968, Owen is in Phoenix where he is performing his duty of notifying the families of fallen soldiers. He calls John to meet him there, and John is unaware that Owen expects to die. Later John finds out from Owen's journal that the only thing that confused him about his death was the location because he was sure it was to be saving Vietnamese children, but he has never been deployed. John and Owen hang out together by the pool for a couple days and meeting the family of the soldier who has died; they are pretty trashy and the fifteen year old brother of the, Dick Jarvits, carries a machete and dreams of going to war. The day Owen expects to die he and Major Rawls accompany John to the airport for his flight home. At the airport, Owen sees some nuns get off the plane with some Vietnamese boys who Owen accompanies to the rest room, followed by John. Suddenly Dick Jarvits appears toting a machete and a grenade, which he throws into the room of screaming kids. John catches the grenade and Owen asks him if he understands why they spent so much time practicing their slam-dunk move now. John tosses the grenade to Owen, lifts him up, and carries him to the window where he smothers the grenade with his body. Owen's arms are ripped off in the blast, and his body is flung back into the sink where a nun rushes to his aid. Dick Jarvits is killed with his own machete by Major Rawls.

John finally realizes that Owen was placed on Earth for this specific job. He was small, so the children would trust him, and his voice was high, so the kids would not be frightened; he was truly an instrument of God just as he thought. Owen had even written "Phoenix" in his journal, knowing that would be where he died. John has, from this moment on, seen Owen Meany as a miracle and as proof of God's existence.

About BookCaps

We all need refreshers every now and then. Whether you are a student trying to cram for that big final, or someone just trying to understand a book more, BookCaps can help. We are a small, but growing company, and are adding titles every month.

Visit www.bookcaps.com to see more of our books, or contact us with any questions.

Made in the USA
Middletown, DE
07 August 2017